COACH W
OF SUC

Coach Wooden is ... known in the profes... ...he took great players and molded them into national champions with a sprinkling of overachievers is spectacular. When I read his book, I knew exactly where he got his wisdom.

John's confidence, poise, communication skills and patience come from the Lord. He allowed these to enfold him, and the results show in this book.

BOBBY BOWDEN
HEAD FOOTBALL COACH, FLORIDA STATE UNIVERSITY

Reading *Coach Wooden's Pyramid of Success* by Jay Carty and Coach Wooden made me feel like I was back at Coach's home, when a warm, peaceful feeling would come over me as I listened to Coach talk in his easy manner. Jay brings together Coach's faith and hard work and intertwines them with principles from the Bible. Just like Coach, this book is easy to be with, and reading it brings a sense of peace.

ANN MEYERS DRYSDALE
UCLA ALL-AMERICAN
HALL OF FAMER
OLYMPIAN

This truly inspirational book shows us how Coach Wooden has used his faith as a cornerstone to live his life. Like the great teacher and coach that he is, Coach Wooden challenges us to evaluate where we stand on fundamental principles and gives us guidance to improve in these areas of our lives.

RUTH RILEY
WNBA DETROIT SHOCK
2004 OLYMPIC GOLD MEDALIST

THE FOUNDATION
OF A LEGEND

I have always admired John Wooden, not only for his success on the basketball court, but also for his success in creating a legacy of excellence and integrity. When you are in the public eye you are under a great deal of scrutiny, and it is easy to make a major mistake or two. Over all these years, Coach Wooden has upheld his character and ideals in an admirable way. When he is remembered, thoughts will be drawn toward his teams, his attitude and his love for his wife and family.

John Wooden will also be remembered for his teaching ability. They don't call him "Coach" for nothing. His Pyramid of Success has been the cornerstone of his teaching for many years.

In this book, Coach Wooden and Jay Carty take you through Scriptures and show you the tremendous practicality of Scriptures in your life today. They show you how to use God's Word to build a solid foundation in your life for whatever you do.

All good and lasting success is based on how we relate to God and how we relate to our fellow man. I hope that as you read this book, you will begin to understand what has served as the foundation for a great sportsman and a great human being.

David Robinson
San Antonio Spurs, 1989-2003
Two-Time NBA World Champion

INTRODUCTION

A playbook is a game plan. It is a scheme to help players and teams perform at their best. Whether the endeavor is in basketball or life itself, the participant needs an action plan.

A football playbook is thick and complex. It contains every offensive and defensive play for eleven players. A basketball playbook, tracking just five players, may fill only a few pages. An individual sport playbook—if it has one at all—may be no longer than a single page.

Some playbooks contain scouting reports on the next opponent and include tips on ways to minimize the other team's strengths and take advantage of its weaknesses. It often analyzes each opposing player.

A coach who chooses to have a playbook uses it to communicate winning strategies to his players. God, too, has a winning strategy. He communicates it through His playbook, the Bible. He lays out the fundamentals and details of what He wants His followers to do. He has also scouted the opposition and formulated a game plan. To achieve victory, all we have to do is read it and act upon what we read.

Drawing from the Pyramid of Success and from God's playbook, the Bible, we have put together this playbook for a successful life. The readings are condensed from the larger book, *Coach Wooden's Pyramid of Success*.

What you find here is the tip of the iceberg, but there is enough to point you in the right direction. Each day we examine a point from the Pyramid, and then provide an opportunity to apply it. To best use this book, take time to answer the questions at the end of each section and take advantage of the journaling space to examine and improve your own life. We have intentionally left extra space so that you can customize this playbook.

To thrive, we all need a game plan. This playbook is one tool that will help you climb the pyramid to a successful life.

THE PYRAMID

JOHN R. WOODEN

Head Basketball Coach, Emeritus
UCLA

FAITH (through prayer)

FIGHT (determined effort)

RESOURCEFULNESS (proper judgment)

ADAPTABILITY (to any situation)

AMBITION (for noble goals)

COMPETITIVE GREATNESS
Be at your best when your best is needed.

POISE
Just being yourself. Being at ease in any situation. Never fighting yourself.

CONDITION
Mental-Moral-Physical. Rest, exercise and diet must be considered. Moderation must be practiced. Dissipation must be eliminated.

SKILL
A knowledge of and the ability to properly and quickly execute the fundamentals.

SELF-CONTROL
Practice self-discipline and keep emotions under control. Good judgment and common sense are essential.

ALERTNESS
Be observing constantly. Stay open minded. Be eager to learn and improve.

INDUSTRIOUSNESS
There is no substitute for work. Worthwhile results come from hard work and careful planning.

FRIENDSHIP
Comes from mutual esteem, respect and devotion. Like marriage, it must not be taken for granted but requires a joint effort.

LOYALTY
To yourself and to all those depending upon you.

OF SUCCESS™

PATIENCE
(good things take time)

Enjoyment of a difficult challenge.

INTEGRITY
(purity of intention)

Success is peace of mind which is a direct result of self-satisfaction in knowing you did your best to become the best that you are capable of becoming.

RELIABILITY
(creates respect)

CONFIDENCE
Respect without fear. May come from being prepared and keeping all things in proper perspective.

Be prepared and cover every little detail.

TEAM SPIRIT
A genuine consideration for others. An eagerness to sacrifice personal interests or glory for the welfare of all.

HONESTY
(in thought and action)

INITIATIVE
Cultivate the ability to make decisions and think alone. Do not be afraid of failure, but learn from it.

INTENTNESS
Set a realistic goal. Concentrate on its achievement by resisting all temptations and being determined and persistent.

SINCERITY
(keeps friends)

Keep your self-respect.

COOPERATION
With all levels of your coworkers. Listen if you want to be heard. Be interested in finding the best way, not in having your own way.

ENTHUSIASM
Brushes off upon those with whom you come in contact. You must truly enjoy what you are doing.

INDUSTRIOUSNESS (HARD WORK)

WOODEN

Industriousness has two components—work and planning. Let's start with work.

There is no substitute for hard work. If we look for shortcuts or the easiest way to complete any given task, we will only put out a minimum effort. We might get by for a while, but in the long run we won't fully develop our talents.

As a basketball player, I wanted to be in the best possible physical condition. There was a time when I'd tell myself, *I'm going to be in better condition than anyone else.* As I grew older, my thinking changed to, *I'm going to be in the best possible condition I can be in.* I had learned that I only have control over myself.

Off the court, I worked hard, too. As head basketball coach at UCLA, each year, a couple of weeks after our last game, I would begin research on some aspect of the sport. I would talk with other coaches, read books and examine every angle of that year's topic. My research would last for the entire off-season.

Nowadays my bad knees and bad hips make it difficult to walk very far or to stand for very long, but I keep up with a busy schedule. Even at 94, I want to be the best I can be, and hard work is the only way to make this happen.

Good planning and hard work lead to prosperity, but hasty shortcuts lead to poverty (Prov. 21:5).

CARTY

Most people slack off when they think that their shortcut or lack of effort will go undetected. However, there is someone who is always looking. God sees us every minute of every day, and He wants us to work with an attitude of doing everything we do as a gift to Him.

The apostle Paul is a great example of a hard worker. He displayed the trait both before he was a Christian and after he became a believer. In his pre-Christian days, he was known as Saul, the relentless persecutor of the Church (see Acts 8:1-3). As Paul, he endured great hardship to plant churches in many lands (see 2 Cor. 11:23-27). He even paid his own way, working as a tentmaker. Paul reminded people, "Don't you remember, dear brothers and sisters, how hard we worked among you?" (1 Thess. 2:9).

Being an apostle was hard work, but Paul loved it. He didn't work for people or for himself; he worked for God's glory (see 1 Cor. 10:31). When we follow Paul's example, it's easier to give our all. Recognizing hard work as a gift to the Lord is the cornerstone to becoming all we are capable of becoming.

INDUSTRIOUSNESS (HARD WORK)

There is no substitute for work. Worthwhile results come from hard work and careful planning.

Your Turn

■ Read Proverbs 13:4,11; 14:23; 22:29; 28:19; 31:13-27; and Ephesians 6:7.

■ On Coach's path to excellence, he chose an aspect of the game and studied it thoroughly. Make a list of issues in your life that need some hard work. Choose one area and establish a plan to develop excellence. Who will you contact? What will you read? What will you do?

❑ I commit myself to a lifestyle of hard work so that I can become all God created me to be.

*Heavenly Father, help me to view the effort
I give in every aspect of my life as a gift to You.
Lord, teach me to work for You and not for people.
I want to fulfill the plans You have for me—
for Your glory. Thank You.*

INDUSTRIOUSNESS (PLANNING)

WOODEN

Undirected diligence isn't very efficient; therefore, some planning must go into hard work. The combination of the two produces industriousness.

As coach at UCLA, I spent two hours with my staff planning each practice. Each drill was calculated to the minute. Every aspect of the session was choreographed, including where the practice balls would be placed. I did not want any time lost by players running to a misplaced ball bin.

Practice under some coaches runs for three hours. Mine lasted an hour and a half to two hours, and we always finished on time. If practice does not end when it is supposed to end, players will hold back a little effort and energy. I wanted my players to give their best effort throughout practice, so I became a stickler for time management. As a result, my players knew how long practice would run and worked harder during the scheduled time. By having practices carefully orchestrated and always ending on time, we got more done in a shorter period of time.

If we are going to become all that we are capable of becoming, we need to work hard, but we also need to be *intentional* about the hard work. Planning places effort where effort is most needed. People who combine these two components have a firm cornerstone of industriousness upon which they can build toward success.

Good planning and hard work lead to prosperity, but hasty shortcuts lead to poverty (Prov. 21:5).

CARTY

God is sovereign and He has plans for each of us (see Pss. 33:11; 40:5; Jer. 29:11). He will sometimes even help us dream up plans (see the story about Joseph in Gen. 41). Such an arrangement seems simple enough until we consider that He also gives us free will and He expects us to make plans.

How can we go about making plans? Proverbs provides practical instruction: "Commit your work to the LORD, and then your plans will succeed" (16:3). There, however, is a caveat: "You can make many plans, but the Lord's purpose will prevail" (Prov. 19:21).

This is an old lesson. A long time ago, some people planned to build a monument to their own greatness. They designed it to reach into heaven and it was to be called the Tower of Babel. However, since the people were trying to worship themselves rather than God, God stopped the project. He scrambled the language of the people of that day and scattered them to the ends of the earth (see Gen. 11:4-6).

When proper planning falls in line with the Lord's purpose, hard work becomes efficient and productive. Coach calls this industriousness, a cornerstone in the Pyramid of Success.

INDUSTRIOUSNESS (PLANNING)

There is no substitute for work. Worthwhile results come from hard work and careful planning.

YOUR TURN

■ Read Genesis 11:4-6; 41:46-57; Psalms 33:11; 40:5; Jeremiah 29:11; Luke 14:28; and 1 Corinthians 15:58.

■ Make a list of the activities you do each week. Estimate the time spent on each activity. Does the time spent reflect the amount of time you'd like to spend? Do you start and end on time? What changes do you need to make to better manage your time and become more industrious?

❑ I commit myself to establishing and maintaining a time of reflection.

Lord God, thank You for the plans You have for me. Thank You that they are plans for welfare and not calamity. Guide me in making my plans an outward expression of Your plans. Show me the value of combining hard work with careful planning that I might be more efficient in furthering Your Kingdom. Thank You.

ENTHUSIASM

WOODEN

If we are to succeed, we have to enjoy what we do. If we enjoy what we do, we will be enthusiastic about it. Enthusiasm thereby enables us to push as hard as we need to push for as long as we need to push to achieve our best.

Regardless of the task, leaders who expect those under their supervision to work near their respective levels of competency must be enthusiastic and enjoy the task at hand. With few exceptions, unenthusiastic leaders keep those under their charge from achieving their collective best.

As beneficial as enthusiasm is, it must be dispatched in moderation. Extreme highs do not work. In fact, too much emotion can be counterproductive. Highs lead to lows, and such swings of intensity result in instability. I wanted my players on an even keel so that their thinking wasn't adversely affected by emotion. Quiet enthusiasm gets results. It exudes confidence and rubs off in wonderful ways.

Even in retirement, I am enthusiastic about most tasks—and I am now busier than ever. However, some responsibilities can still become drudgery—that's when I risk losing my enthusiasm. We're more productive and come closer to being all we can be when we do the tasks we like to do.

Never be lazy in your work, but serve the Lord enthusiastically (Rom. 12:11).

CARTY

Apollos was enthusiastic, but there was a problem. He understood and taught Old Testament Scriptures, and even taught accurately about Jesus—but he only went as far as John's baptism. His enthusiasm was rubbing off, but he wasn't giving people the whole picture.

When Apollos arrived in Ephesus, Priscilla and Aquila heard his bold preaching and saw a diamond in the rough. They took Apollos aside and explained things to him more accurately. Apollos took good notes. When he went on to Achaia, "He refuted all the Jews with powerful arguments in public debate. Using the Scriptures, he explained to them, 'The Messiah you are looking for is Jesus'" (Acts 18:28). Apollos preached with enthusiasm. It was his passion for the Word that set him apart and his humility that kept him straight.

Biblical enthusiasm means to boil in the spirit, to commit with your whole heart and to be zealous and passionate. God wants us to be that way about Him and His Son, and He wants us to be that way about becoming all that He designed us to be. Enthusiasm is a cornerstone in the Pyramid of Success, but when it comes to faith, it must be coupled with knowledge.

ENTHUSIASM
Brushes off with those with whom you come in contact. You must truly enjoy what you are doing.

YOUR TURN

■ Read Psalm 42:1-2; Ecclesiastes 12:1; Acts 18:24-28; 1 Corinthians 1:12; 3:4-6; 4:6; Galatians 6:9; and Revelation 2:4.

■ List the three responsibilities in your life that you enjoy the most and the three that you enjoy the least. How does your level of enthusiasm differ when approaching your most favorite tasks as compared to your least favorite tasks? How can you avoid drudgery and become more enthusiastic about everyday jobs? What can you do to keep your enthusiasm under control and quietly rub off on others?

❑ I commit myself to a lifestyle of enthusiasm.

Almighty God of excitement and passion, I want to serve You with my whole heart and every fiber of my being. Give me a passion for Your Son that will rub off on all whom You place in my path and the knowledge and understanding to be firm in my faith. Father, I want to become all that I can become as Your enthusiastic representative. May it be so.

FRIENDSHIP

WOODEN

The three blocks between the cornerstones are the "people blocks" of friendship, loyalty and cooperation. People make us better. It is easier to reach our potential when we learn the value of including others in our quest. We can accomplish so much more when we work with others.

If we are going to successfully work with others, it is vital to know the function of friendship. After all, God created us to be dependent upon each other.

Friendship comes from mutual esteem and devotion. Friendship is doing for others while they are doing for us. It's called ministry when all of the doing goes one direction. Friendship goes both ways. Friendship is like a good marriage—it's based on common concern. Friends help each other; they don't use each other.

If we are concerned about being successful in the eyes of others, our reputation may be fine, but our character is suspect. Our reputation is what we're perceived to be; our character is what we really are. We should be more concerned about our character than our reputation. A good reputation is not worth much if we have faulty character. If we use our friends to advance a personal agenda, we'll never have inner peace.

Friends help to complete us, and we'll be better for having taken them along on our journey to becoming all we are capable of becoming.

A person standing alone can be attacked and defeated, but two can stand back-to-back and conquer. Three are even better, for a triple-braided cord is not easily broken (Eccles. 4:12).

Carty

The Bible contains much about friendship. Ruth and her mother-in law were tight (see Ruth 1:16). David and Jonathan were close (see 1 Sam. 18:3). Job's friends consoled him when he lost everything (see 2:11).

In Daniel, we read about three Jewish men who were friends. Shadrach, Meshach and Abednego were so close that they even faced death together when King Nebuchadnezzar threw them into the fiery furnace. What would have happened if the three hadn't had each other? Individually, would they have caved in to save their respective skins? Who knows? But we do know that collectively they formed a triple-braided cord that could not easily be broken.

Do you have friends who push you toward becoming the best you can be? If not, you should meet regularly with some same-gender friends and ask each other hard questions about things such as lust, greed and anger. Hold each other accountable. Prod each other toward becoming all that each one of you is capable of becoming.

FRIENDSHIP

Comes from mutual esteem,
respect and devotion. Like marriage,
it must not be taken for granted but
requires a joint effort.

YOUR TURN

■ Read Daniel 3:3—4:3; Proverbs 17:17; 18:24;
1 Corinthians 13:4-7; John 15:13; and
Philippians 2:3.

■ Based on biblical examples of friendship,
make a list of the people in your life who
would qualify as your friends. Who on that
list do you trust the most? How could you
go about establishing accountability with
that person or persons?

❑ I commit myself to being accountable.

*Dear Author of friendship, I thank You that I can
have You as a friend through Jesus Christ my Lord.
Please send a few good friends my way so that I can
be part of a three-strand cord of strength and bring
more glory to Your Name. Use me to help them and
them to help me faithfully walk with You. Thank You.*

COOPERATION

WOODEN

Cooperation is working with others for the benefit of all. It is not sacrificing for someone else's benefit. If our actions don't help everyone involved, what we are doing is something other than cooperation—perhaps it is ministry, service or selfishness.

Some individuals, such as writers and scientists, often work alone and accomplish much. But in my opinion, those who primarily work alone will never become all they could become if they were working in cooperation with others. Working as part of a team makes us much more than we could ever be alone.

When I was a young boy, I was at a gravel pit with my father and a young man. They had a team of horses and were attempting to pull a load up a steep road. The young man driving the horses was loud and abusive. In response, the animals were agitated, worked against each other and couldn't pull the load. With a gentle voice and a gentler touch, my dad calmed the horses and walked them forward with the load.

I learned two important lessons that day: (1) gentleness is a better method of getting cooperation than harshness, and (2) a team can accomplish much more when it works together than individuals can when they work alone.

Two people can accomplish more than twice as much as one; they get a better return for their labor (Eccles. 4:9).

CARITY

Paul and Peter sought to stimulate the use of spiritual gifts among the team of believers in the New Testament Church. Paul wrote, "Just as our bodies have many parts and each part has a special function, so it is with Christ's body. We are all parts of his one body, and each of us has different work to do" (Rom. 12:4-5). In other words, in God's design, we need to cooperate.

More than 20 gifts are noted in the New Testament (see Rom. 12:3-8; 1 Cor. 12:1-11; Eph. 4:7-16). However, many Bible scholars do not think that the list is exhaustive. Every believer is given at least one gift (see 1 Pet. 4:10).

A problem arises when a believer doesn't use his or her gift (see 1 Thess. 5:19). Cooperation is stifled, and the team suffers. Just as the physical body hurts when an organ doesn't function, so it is when a member of the Body of Christ chooses not to cooperate.

We need partners to maximize our spiritual potential. Corporate efforts add to the Body of Christ in ways well beyond what could ever be accomplished by individuals alone.

COOPERATION

With all levels of your coworkers. Listen if you want to be heard. Be interested in finding the best way, not in having your own way.

YOUR TURN

■ Read 1 Chronicles 9:22-34; Psalm 84:10; Ecclesiastes 4:9-12; Romans 12:3-8; Ephesians 4:7-16; 1 Corinthians 12:1-11; 1 Peter 4:10; 1 Thessalonians 5:19; and Revelation 4:8.

■ List some key contexts where you find yourself in a cooperative group and where you find yourself alone.

❑ I commit myself to developing a team spirit in all I do.

Dear Lord God, You are the author of interdependency. You gave us a need for each other. Give me a willingness to cooperate with my brothers and sisters in Christ. Maximize our spiritual potential so as to bring greater glory to Your name. Thank You.

LOYALTY

WOODEN

When I played basketball at Purdue University, I wore my hair rather short and close-cropped. Some youngsters who followed our team wanted to wear their hair the same way. My haircut was known as the Putnamville bob, and many boys who also wore it that way were loyal fans. Today, youngsters often wear certain clothes or listen to certain music because NBA players do.

Loyalty, however, is more than emulating someone's looks, wardrobe or music. That is attachment or identification. True loyalty comes into play when we add concepts such as devotion, duty, faithfulness and commitment. These virtues can be given to people, teams, organizations, governments, countries, ideals, rulers, religions or God.

Loyalty is the foundational quality that gets us through hard times. Will we compromise our integrity when temptation is great or the going gets rough? Or will we remain loyal to our beliefs and core values?

In basketball, we want to know if we can count on our teammates. When we know that they will be there to support us in tight spots, we are more likely to go the extra mile when they also need help. That combination makes each of us better. Loyalty is the force that forges individuals into a team. It's the component that moves teams toward great achievements. No individual or team will become great without loyalty.

So then, brethren, stand firm and hold to the traditions which you were taught, whether by word of mouth or by letter from us (2 Thess. 2:15, *NASB*).

CARTY

Check out 1 Chronicles 11:10-37. It's okay to skim through the list of names, but look at the stories. Jashobeam killed 300 men with just a spear (see 1 Chron. 11:11), and some guys broke through the Philistine lines just to get David a drink. What David did with the drink will amaze you (see 1 Chron. 11:18-19)

David was loyal to his men, and his men were so loyal to him that they made him their king. David's men were also loyal to each other. Uriah the Hittite was on the front lines fighting the Ammonites. When he was the only one called home, he was so loyal to his fellow fighters that he declined the pleasures his wife and home had to offer. If his mates couldn't enjoy their homes, he refused to enjoy his.

God wants us to be like David's men. He wants us to make Him king in our lives. He wants us to advance His Kingdom and be ready to put our lives on the line, if the need arises. God definitely demands that we be loyal to Him and to each other. This fact alone makes this a vital building block in the Pyramid.

LOYALTY

*To yourself and to all those depending upon you.
Keep your self-respect.*

Your Turn

■ Read 1 Chronicles 11:10—12:37; 2 Samuel 11:2-13; Numbers 32:6-18; Hebrews 13:8; 2 Thessalonians 2:13-15; and James 1:17.

■ Recount times when you made a commitment to be loyal to someone and it proved costly. Recall one time when you depended on someone to be loyal to you and he or she failed. Describe the emotions you felt at that time and afterward regarding the incident and the person.

❑ I commit myself to a lifestyle of being loyal to my family, my colleagues, my friends, my spouse and those to whom I have given my word.

Oh God, I want You and You alone to be my God. I offer You everything I have, including my devotion and loyalty. May I faithfully carry out my responsibilities in Your Kingdom and my responsibilities to all believers. With all my heart, I want my loyalty to pass the tests and temptations that will be coming my way. Give me strength to stand firm. Thank You.

SELF-CONTROL

WOODEN

Self-control is the ability to discipline ourselves and keep our emotions under control. To become our best, good judgment and common sense are essential. No matter the task—whether physical or mental—if our emotions take over, we're not going to execute near our personal level of competency, because both judgment and common sense will be impaired. When our emotions dominate our actions, we make mistakes.

A lack of self-control not only hinders individual achievement, it inhibits team accomplishment. For example, when disciplining someone we supervise, if our emotions take over, chances are we're going to antagonize that person. It's difficult to get productive, positive results under these circumstances. We must remember why we discipline. We do it to help, to prevent, to correct and to improve, but not to punish. It takes self-control to accomplish this goal.

To this day, I honestly feel that every one of my 10 national championship teams demonstrated more self-control than any other team I've ever seen. In every championship game when we had the game won, during a timeout I directed the players, "Don't make fools out of yourselves. Let's let the alumni and the fans do that. I know you want to get the nets and I know you feel good, and that's fine, but let's have no excessive exultation." Each of my championship teams won with class, and I'm proud of that.

Knowing God leads to self-control. Self-control leads to patient endurance, and patient endurance leads to godliness (2 Pet. 5:6).

CARTY

Coach Wooden would have been proud of Joseph. The lad had class and self-control (see Judg. 7:12). Having been sold into slavery, Joseph moved up to become the number one honcho in Potiphar's house. Potiphar was the captain of Pharaoh's personal bodyguards.

Joseph was handsome and well built. Potiphar's wife noticed. She must have been a bored, rich, desperate housewife looking for a boy-toy. One day she invited Joseph into her bedroom. Joseph was surely tempted, but he exercised self control and chose to stay pure.

Since Potiphar's wife couldn't have Joseph, she decided to trash him—she claimed that he tried to rape her. As a result, Potiphar threw Joseph in jail. Joseph had self-control. He didn't let sexual inducement overcome him, and he didn't throw an emotional fit at God when he lost everything. Joseph never allowed his common sense to be compromised. Instead, he let the cream rise to the top and started running the prison. Because Joseph displayed self-control and faithfulness, God blessed him. Ultimately, Joseph became Pharaoh's right-hand man and second in control of Egypt.

> **SELF-CONTROL**
>
> *Practice self-discipline and keep emotions under control. Good judgment and common sense are essential.*

Your Turn

■ Read Genesis 39:1-20; Romans 3:21-30; Galatians 5:16-24; James 3:1-12; and 2 Peter 1:5-11.

■ What areas of your life present the greatest difficulty in gaining and maintaining self-control? Describe two or three encounters in which you have seen your emotions hinder clear thinking.

❑ I commit myself to living a balanced life with greater self-control and sounder judgment.

Oh God of eternal glory, I want all the days of my life to reflect the glory of my Lord Jesus Christ. Help me to overcome temptation so that I might be all I am capable of becoming in honoring Your holy name. Thank You.

JOURNAL ENTRY
BUILDING BLOCK 6: SELF-CONTROL

ALERTNESS

WOODEN

We must be alert. This simply means that we observe what is going on around us. Except for what we garner through personal experience, everything else we learn comes through observation.

My father often reminded me that Abraham Lincoln had said that he had never met a person from whom he did not learn something, although most of the time it was something not to do. There is a lot of truth in that, but the point is that Lincoln was always observing and alert to what was going on around him, and he was constantly learning.

When we aren't alert, we miss opportunities to improve ourselves. We should always watch for circumstances or situations that can help or harm us and be eager to learn from these encounters.

Too many people narrow their awareness. I wanted my players to always be expanding their awareness and searching, especially for truth. I wanted them to know what they believed and be able to defend it.

I'm not a relativist. I don't think we are supposed to find our own truth. That's playing God. I believe in absolute truth and absolute sin, and the Bible is my standard for determining those absolutes. With that in mind, I believe that an inquisitive person is more apt to discover truth than someone with a closed mind.

So let's not sleepwalk through life like those others. Let's keep our eyes open and be smart (1 Thess. 5:6, *THE MESSAGE*).

CARTY

The Israelites weren't always alert. Sometimes they closed their minds to God and rode a sin cycle. Someone on a sin cycle endures the consequences, repents of the sin, enjoys life for a while, forgets about God, sins again, endures, repents, enjoys, forgets, sins some more, and so on. Once when the Israelites were riding this cycle, to get their attention, God gave them over to their foes—ouch!

What's the big deal about staying alert? God warned us, "Keep a cool head. Stay alert. The Devil is poised to pounce, and would like nothing better than to catch you napping" (1 Pet. 5:8, *THE MESSAGE*). God has given us a scouting report on our adversary. Satan hates God and he wants our souls. If he can't have our souls, he at least wants us on a sin cycle.

If you have been riding a sin cycle, perhaps it's time to stop, ask forgiveness through Jesus Christ, put on the whole armor of God (see Eph. 6:10-20) and move forward. The keys to moving forward in God are staying alert, remaining watchful and filtering everything through His holy Word.

ALERTNESS
*Be observing constantly. Stay open minded.
Be eager to learn and improve.*

Your Turn

■ Read Judges 6:1–7:23; 1 Corinthians 16:13; Ephesians 6:10-20; Colossians 4:2; and 1 Peter 5:8.

■ How alert are you to God's voice? How alert are you to the enemy's plans for your life? Are you riding a sin cycle? What can you change in your life to get off (or stay off) the cycle and become more alert to God?

❑ I commit myself to continue listening to God and learning about Him and His plan for my life.

Holy God of truth and life, forgive me for the cycles of sin that I've allowed in my life. I haven't always been alert to Your leading. I repent. Please guard my heart, ears and eyes from the lies of our adversary. Help me to always be on guard, ever watchful and always alert to his schemes. I want to stand against him and I want to stand firm for You. May it be so.

INITIATIVE

WOODEN

Initiative is having the courage to make decisions and take action. People with initiative move forward without fear of failure, even though they might make mistakes or fail. People with initiative will act when action is needed.

If we allow the fear of failure to keep us from acting, we will never be successful or reach our full potential. Let's face it, we're all imperfect and on occasion we're going to fall short, but we must learn from failure, and that will enable us to avoid repeating our mistakes. Through adversity, we learn, grow stronger and become better people.

My college coach once said, "The team that makes the most mistakes will probably outscore the other one." What he meant is that doers make mistakes, but if we aren't doing anything, we're making the greatest mistake of all.

I wanted my players to be active and to take initiative. I didn't want them worrying about mistakes, as long as they didn't repeat the same ones over and over. I wanted them to learn from their mistakes. I didn't like conservative practices. I expected a certain number of turnovers, but I wanted the right kind. Careless mistakes aren't the right kind. Mistakes made while expanding boundaries are what I wanted. If we weren't pushing against the walls of our capabilities, we weren't practicing correctly, which usually meant we were not taking enough initiative.

He prayed more fervently, and he was in such agony of spirit that his sweat fell to the ground like great drops of blood (Luke 22:44).

CARTY

As graphic as Mel Gibson's *The Passion of the Christ* was, it did not show everything. On the cross, Jesus' face would have been unrecognizable, and most likely His ribs would have been exposed. As bad as this physical pain was, Jesus' greatest challenge was being apart from the Father. Minimally, that's what hell is—complete and total separation from God.

For 12 hours, Jesus was beaten. He eventually took on the weight of all sin and visited hell. How did Jesus prepare for the suffering? He fortified Himself with prayer.

The fact that Jesus sweated blood while He was praying is indicative of the lengths to which He had to go to if He was to overcome the threat of failure. This wasn't a now-I-lay-me-down-to-sleep kind of prayer. Jesus agonized. It was literally a contest between His flesh, satanic temptation and the Father's will.

In the flesh, Jesus didn't want to go through the suffering, but in His heart He wanted to do the Father's will more than His own. Jesus' greater desire overcame the paralysis of fear and initiated the greatest act of love the world has ever seen.

INITIATIVE
Cultivate the ability to make decisions and think alone. Do not be afraid of failure, but learn from it.

Your Turn

- Read Luke 22:39-46; Matthew 26:36-45; John 13:21-30; and Philippians 4:4-9.

- When was the last time that you attempted something new and it didn't work out? How did failure affect you?

- I commit to boldly press the boundaries of my life to reach my greatest potential.

Heavenly Father, help me to overcome the fears of life and look more like Your Son. Give me the courage to make decisions and take the actions that will represent Him and You well. Give me boldness for Jesus Christ. Thank You.

INTENTNESS

WOODEN

I could have called this building block determination or perseverance. I suppose persistence or even tenacity would have been adequate. But intentness embraces all of those words and more, and it best states the final block on the second tier of the Pyramid.

Intentness is the ability to resist temptation and to avoid rabbit trails of distraction. An intent person will stay the course and go the distance. He or she will concentrate on objectives with determination, stamina and resolve. Intentness is the quality that won't permit us to quit or give up, even when our goal is going to take a while to accomplish.

Our society has been permeated by a mindset of immediate gratification. Simply put, people are impatient. They want too much too soon. They have lost sight of an overarching truth: in life, worthwhile accomplishments and acquisitions take time. Usually, the better the reward, the more time it takes to acquire it. Intentness gives us the doggedness to hang in there and overcome impatience. Intentness is patience with action.

Without intentness we can't possibly become all we can be. However, assuming our ability warrants it, we can approach the pinnacle of our profession, position or title if we have the resolve to plow through whatever life throws at us—even if it is a curve.

She thought, "If I can just touch his robe, I will be healed" (Matt. 9:21).

CARTY

During biblical times, Levitical law made life tough for women. For instance, during her period, a woman was considered to be ceremonially unclean. Anyone who touched her would be unclean, and anything she touched was also considered unclean (see Lev. 15:25).

One particular woman's discharge had continued for 12 terrible years. She had visited all the doctors and spent all of her money in search of a cure. Nothing had worked.

One day, Jesus passed her way. He was in the street being thronged. Everyone was trying to touch him. She was weak. There was no way she could force her way through the crowd. But she was intent, so she crawled. The woman thought, *If I can just touch His robe, I will be healed* (see Matt. 9:21).

She barely touched the fringe of the robe, but it was enough. She was healed. The woman had the kind of faith that made her touch different from the others who touched Jesus. Christ was being thronged, but power went out of Him to only one person in the mob. Why? She had determination, perseverance, persistence, tenacity and resolve all rolled up into one all-inclusive word that applied to her faith. She was intent.

INTENTNESS

Set a realistic goal. Concentrate on its achievement by resisting all temptations and being determined and persistent.

YOUR TURN

■ Read Leviticus 15:19-33; Luke 8:43-48; 11:5-13; and Matthew 9:20-23.

■ How do you usually respond to circumstances that could prevent success? Describe a time when you successfully pushed through distractions and difficulties to reach a goal.

❑ I commit myself to be focused on the main objective of reaching excellence and to avoid anything less important that would keep me from reaching my greatest potential.

Almighty healer and author of faith, give me the faith that heals my infirmities, but more than that, give me the faith that heals my soul. Then give me intentness about the things that are important to You. Not my will, but Your will be done, in Jesus' name I pray. Amen.

CONDITION

WOODEN

By condition, I mean physical, mental, moral and spiritual fitness. In any of life's endeavors—not just athletics—rest, exercise, diet and drills only get us so far. Only when we live a wholesome lifestyle will we see the greatest results.

I told my players, "We want to be in the best possible condition." In my early years, I said, "Let's be in better condition than anybody else." But I changed. If the other team had more capacity for conditioning, they might have been better than we were, and there was nothing we could have done about it. So I started saying, "Let's become the best conditioned team we can possibly be. We hope that'll be better than the others, but we don't know if it will be. But let's make the effort to be in the best possible condition with the hope that we'll be the best."

I also told my players about shared responsibility. As coach, my responsibility was to run effective practices. Their responsibility occurred between practices. They understood that a lack of proper conduct, deficient rest and an improper diet would keep them from attaining and maintaining their best possible conditioning. Moreover, they couldn't produce their best without the physical conditioning being preceded by mental, moral and spiritual conditioning. A failure to address mental, moral and spiritual conditioning will limit even the best physical conditioning.

Physical exercise has some value, but spiritual exercise is much more important, for it promises a reward in both this life and the next (1 Tim. 4:8).

CARTY

The most demanding test of my physical conditioning came when I was in college. A teenaged boy was in trouble in a lake about 125 yards out. I got to him as he sank. I had to use a cross-chest carry to ferry him in because he fought me all the way. If I hadn't been in great shape, the boy would have drowned.

My spiritual conditioning is tested all of the time. I've been in the ministry for 30 years, and there is constant temptation to sin. If I didn't maintain my spiritual fitness, I would have been out of the ministry long ago.

The apostle Paul said, "I exercise myself, to have always a conscience void of offense toward God, and toward men" (Acts 24:16, KJV). The word "exercise" means to actively train, practice and struggle to give one's best, even to the point of pain.

For the athlete, physical conditioning is important, but Coach got it right when he said that we won't be a success without mental, moral and spiritual conditioning as well. It's important to be in top condition in all of these areas. When God calls, we need to be ready to respond.

CONDITION

Mental-Moral-Physical. Rest, exercise and diet must be considered. Moderation must be practiced. Dissipation must be eliminated.

Your Turn

■ Read 1 Kings 16:29—18:46 and Acts 24:16.

■ List the things that you do regularly to condition yourself physically, mentally, morally and spiritually.

❑ I commit myself to becoming and staying fit physically, mentally, morally and spiritually.

Holy Father in heaven, I desire to get into the best possible physical, mental, moral and spiritual condition. Help me to use my time wisely, and give me the desire to follow through until I reach my goals. I want to be ready when You call. Thank You.

SKILL

WOODEN

Skill is knowing what to do and being able to execute all of the fundamentals important to a particular task. However, a skillful person usually also has a sense of timing and the ability to quickly perform the skill.

Take driving on a highway as an illustration. We may know how to drive, but if we don't respond quickly to tricky situations, we could be in big trouble. There are countless similar activities in which we must know the fundamentals of a skill and also have the capability to execute the skill properly and quickly.

Any measure of competency requires a command of the fundamentals of a given endeavor. Even a person with limited competency can become at least somewhat skillful if he or she works on the fundamentals. The greater the competency, the more precise a person must be in carrying out the fundamentals.

Obviously, we can't do much about our height or our I.Q.; however, we can affect our brainpower and physical potential through education, training and practice. God only made one Kareem Abdul-Jabbar, one Mother Teresa and one Mel Gibson. The rest of us didn't receive as much potential, but each of us can still become successful. We might not become as significant as we aspire to be, but we can become the best we are capable of becoming.

Do you see any truly competent work-
ers? They will serve kings rather than
ordinary people (Prov. 22:29).

CARTY

Becoming skillful takes time and hard work.
Knowing where to invest that time and work
becomes vital. Who wants to work diligently
but end up not making much of a contribution
with his or her life?

Not discovering our God-given talent mix
early in life is both aggravating and disappoint-
ing. Each of us senses that we are here for a purpose, and we realize that God has plans for us.
Therefore, every day wasted delays the fulfill-
ment that comes from doing what we have been
naturally wired to do.

Our potential for excellence lies in our
undeveloped areas of skill—what I call our God-
given hard wiring, or knack. The primary word
for wisdom in the Bible best translates to "know
your knack." God gives the potential to be skillful. It is our job to discover our potential (the
beginning of wisdom) and develop our talent to
our A+ level of competency (wisdom and success). People who are biblically wise know their
God-given wiring and go forward in developing
their skills. I believe the Bible teaches that each
of us has been given the potential to make a significant contribution to God's kingdom.

SKILL
*A knowledge of and the ability to properly and
quickly execute the fundamentals. Be prepared
and cover every little detail.*

Your Turn

- Read Exodus 28:3; 31:3; 35:10,25,35; 36:1; 1 Kings 7:14; 1 Chronicles 22:15; 28:21; 2 Chronicles 2:7; 26:15; 1 Corinthians 3:10; and Ephesians 5:16.

- Apart from sleeping, list the top five activities in which you spend most of your time. After each letter below, circle the one phrase that best describes you.

    A. People drain me, people energize me or I prefer small groups.

    B. I communicate best with spoken words, written words or artistic expression.

    C. I like working with things or ideas.

    D. I am most skilled at working with my hands, solving problems, selling things or teaching others.

    Measure the time spent in your top five time-consuming activities against the choices above. Are you spending most of your time doing what seems to come naturally?

- ❑ I commit myself to developing and using the talents and gifts God has given me.

*Dear Giver of skills and gifts, show me the area of
service for which You have designed me to best fit,
and direct me to the place where You want me to
serve. I want to develop my skills for You. Most of all,
regardless of my place in the world's hierarchy, give
me the attitude of a servant. Thank You.*

**JOURNAL ENTRY
BUILDING BLOCK 11: SKILL**

TEAM SPIRIT

WOODEN

I once heard team spirit defined as a willingness to lose oneself in the group for the good of the group. I used that definition for a long time, but always thought it fell short. It took a while but I finally figured it out. I changed "willingness" to "eagerness." Willingness is more like "I will if I have to." Eagerness communicates an attitude of "I'll be happy to sacrifice personal accomplishments for the good of the team."

When we *willingly* perform a task that we should or must do for the good of the group, our heart isn't completely in it. This slight reluctance holds back our teammates. By contrast, when every member of a team *eagerly* performs every task, the group rises to a new level of accomplishment.

Team spirit is the ultimate expression of interdependence. Just as team spirit embraces an element of enthusiasm, it also houses a component of cooperation. But where cooperation makes others better, team spirit makes the group better.

Team spirit is consideration, respect and dignity for others. I believe that if heads of state throughout this troubled world of ours truly had more consideration for others, our problems would not be as severe. I'm not saying we wouldn't be without problems. Trouble will always exist. But if we display true consideration for others, most of our problems will be manageable.

If one part suffers, all the parts suffer with it, and if one part is honored, all the parts are glad. Now all of you together are Christ's body, and each one of you is a separate and necessary part of it (1 Cor. 12:26-27).

CARTY

In the Body of Christ, no one role is more important than another (see 1 Cor. 3:7-8). God wants us to know that the evangelist isn't any more significant than the person who disciples another, nor is the one who prepares the soil more valuable than the one who harvests. People who have heard me preach often refer to my contribution as fertilizer. The point is, to God my contribution is no more valuable than yours, but neither is it less.

The apostle Paul emphasized team spirit, noting, "Some of us are Jews, some are Gentiles, some are slaves, and some are free. But we have all been baptized into Christ's body by one Spirit, and we have all received the same Spirit" (1 Cor. 12:13). In some households, the master was being discipled by his slave, and Gentiles were discipling Jews—for the culture of the day, absurd considerations that were outside the concept of team spirit. But God obviously approved.

We cannot think more highly of ourselves than we ought, but neither should we think less of ourselves. We should be eager team members.

TEAM SPIRIT

A genuine consideration for others. An eagerness to sacrifice personal interests of glory for the welfare of all.

Your Turn

- Read John 15:12; Romans 12:3-5,10; 1 Corinthians 3:6-9; 12:12-27; 1 Thessalonians 3:12; and 1 Peter 1:22.

- List the groups to which you belong (e.g., church, parachurch, community, school). What role do you play in each group? Do your current roles best utilize your spiritual gifts and natural talents?

- ❑ I commit myself to finding the best avenue for maximizing my contribution as an enthusiastic member of the Body of Christ.

Almighty Creator, You made us to best function interdependently. Give me an eagerness to contribute my talents and gifts to Your body of believers that we might function as a team and accomplish more for the Kingdom collectively than we could ever accomplish individually. Thank You.

POISE

WOODEN

Most people think of poise as calm, self-assured dignity, but I call it "just being you." When we have poise, we're not acting, faking or pretending. We're not trying to be something we're not, nor are we attempting to live up to others' expectations. Therefore, when we are being who we really are, we'll have a greater likelihood of functioning nearer our own level of competency.

Poise greatly depends upon two nearby blocks: confidence and self-control. Confidence comes from thorough preparation and enables us to be quietly in control at all times. The discipline of self-control usually produces poise.

We acquire poise by being industrious, by being enthusiastic, by being friendly, by being loyal, by being cooperative, by maintaining self-control, by being alert and alive and constantly observant, by having initiative and not being afraid to fail while realizing that we are imperfect and we will fail on occasion, by being intent and determined to reach realistic objectives, by being competitive in whatever we're doing, by being in the best possible condition for whatever we're doing, by being skilled and able to execute not only properly but quickly, and by being imbued with team spirit and consideration for others.

Poise and the next block, confidence, will be the natural outgrowth of having the lower blocks in their proper place. We won't have either unless we also have the others.

I have lifted the yoke of slavery from your neck so you can walk free with your heads held high (Lev. 26:13).

CARITY

Many biblical characters demonstrated calm, assured dignity. In every case, they obtained their poise from God, not through their own efforts. When God's got you, you don't have to trust yourself or be concerned about what anyone else thinks.

Moses, for example, had herded sheep for 40 years, but he wasn't worried about what Pharaoh thought. Moses even had a speech impediment, which is perhaps why he balked before first going to talk to the ruler (see Exod. 4:10). Nonetheless, after confessing his weakness, Moses stood up to the monarch 10 times and demanded that Pharaoh let the Jewish people go.

Moses demonstrated a remarkable combination of control and confidence—the primary components in poise. He displayed courage, too. When those components are rooted in God, rather than self, we have a far firmer foundation upon which to achieve success. For believers, the yoke of the slavery of sin has been lifted. That means we can walk with our heads held high, regardless of our backgrounds (see Lev. 26:13). The confidence that comes from knowing that we're forgiven will also contribute to our poise.

POISE

Just being yourself. Being at ease in any situation. Never fighting yourself.

Your Turn

■ Read: Exodus 4:10; 5:1; Joshua 2:1-21; 6:15-25; and Esther.

■ To answer the following questions, rate yourself on a scale of one to ten by circling the number that best fits you.

· Do you usually spend adequate time in preparation, or do you usually wing it?

Prepare   1 2 3 4 5 6 7 8 9 10   **Wing it**

· When it comes to your relationship with God, are you poised, or are you a poser?

Poised   1 2 3 4 5 6 7 8 9 10   **Posing**

Based on the above self-evaluation, what do you need to work on most?

❑ I will continue to pursue excellence in the qualities that will produce poise in all aspects of my life.

*Almighty Creator of ultimate courage,
I place my confidence in You and my faith in
Christ. I want to be controlled by Your Holy Spirit.
Give me the poise that comes with leading a
Spirit-controlled life. Thank You, blessed Lord.*

CONFIDENCE

WOODEN

Poise and confidence come with proper preparation. When we are as prepared as we know how to be and know that we have the tools to handle most of the unknowns that might come our way, we can go into an event, a job, a meeting, a show or any other venture with total confidence.

I always wanted my teams to be confident, but not over-confident. I did not want them to be cocky or whistling in the dark. Solid respect without fear is what I was after. I wanted them to believe in themselves without being self-centered, intimidated or naive.

I wanted my teams to go onto the floor with style and confidence. Our assuredness needed to so take over the arena that our opponent and the crowd would wonder how we could be so well prepared and so sure of our performance, even before the game started.

I learned to call the plays that would give us the best odds of success. Of course, I never knew if the decision would work, but I did know that over time we would succeed more often if we played the odds. As a result, I had more confidence as a coach, and my players had confidence, too. They knew that we would always be in a position that gave them the best opportunity to do their best as a team.

For I am convinced that neither death, nor life, nor angels, nor principalities, nor things present, nor things to come, nor powers, nor height, nor depth, nor any other created thing, will be able to separate us from the love of God, which is in Christ Jesus our Lord (Rom. 8:38-39, *NASB*).

CARTY

Stephen was a picture of confidence. He was one of the first of seven Early Church deacons. When local Pharisees debated him, they lost—big time. In retaliation, they got false witnesses to testify against him and then put him on trial. During the trial, Stephen delivered what many consider to be the best defense of the faith ever (see Acts 7:2-56). After he had delivered his speech, Stephen was stoned to death.

Stephen had been selected as a deacon because he was of good reputation, was filled with the Holy Spirit and displayed wisdom (see Acts 6:3). When he preached, he demonstrated grace and power, and through him the Holy Spirit performed great wonders and signs (see Acts 6:8). When accused, he remained confident in his faith (see Acts 6:15). No wonder he exhibited confidence. In fact, Stephen was confident that he was going to heaven, and he said so just before the last rock hit him (see Acts 7:59).

CONFIDENCE

Respect without fear. May come from being prepared and keeping all things in proper perspective.

Your Turn

■ Read Acts 6:1—8:3; 22:19-20; Romans 5:1-5; 8:31-39; 1 Corinthians 2:1-5; and 1 John 5:13-15.

■ On a scale of 1 to 10, how convinced are you that nothing will be able to separate you from the love of God, which is in Christ Jesus your Lord? On a scale of 1 to 10, when presented with an opportunity to share your faith, how often do you come through? On a scale of 1 to 10, how convinced are you that your sin is really forgiven?

❑ I commit myself to regularly reading God's Word and to living in the confidence of God's forgiveness by regularly confessing my sins.

Great Giver of confidence and assurance, prepare me with Your Holy Word, fill me with Your Holy Spirit and give me wisdom to confidently turn to You like Stephen did. I know that You will never let me be separated from Your love. Thank You.

COMPETITIVE GREATNESS

WOODEN

If we demonstrate all of the preceding building-block qualities, we have the potential for success, but without competitive greatness, we won't be the best we can be. Competitive greatness is the pinnacle of the Pyramid. With competitive greatness we can deliver our best when our best is needed, and at the same time, we can make those around us better, too. A person with this quality loves a challenge—the tougher the better.

In the sixth game of the 1998 NBA finals, Michael Jordan had the flu, yet he played. During timeouts toward the end of the game he would almost pass out, yet he continued. When he finally won the game—scoring his 45th point with 5.2 seconds to go—he could no longer stand. He was completely spent—he had left it all on the floor. That is competitive greatness.

Having competitive greatness does not always mean that we are the one who scores the most points or hits the winning shot. Lewis Alcindor (Kareem Abdul-Jabbar) could have set every college scoring record in the book, but he didn't. He could see the big picture and always reigned in his own play for the sake of elevating the play of his teammates. As a result, he was rewarded with a championship every year he played.

We don't have to be superstars to reach competitive greatness. All we have to do is learn to rise to every occasion, give our best effort and make those around us better as we do it.

"Don't worry about a thing," David told Saul. "I'll go fight this Philistine!" (1 Sam. 17:32).

CARTY

For Norm Evans, competitive greatness took shape when he played college football under a coach who had much the same outlook as John Wooden. One day after practice, Norm and his coach walked off the field together. The coach put his arm around Norm, looked him in the eye and tenderly said, "Laddie, you didn't give me your best today."

From that day forward, whether in practice or in a game, Norm put out maximum effort. For 14 seasons, Norm was an undersized lineman in the NFL. To survive at that level for so long took competitive greatness. In 1972, he was a vital cog on the offensive line of the undefeated Miami Dolphins. No doubt, his competitive spirit had elevated his play and rubbed off on his teammates, too.

Off the field, we are also in a battle. Have you noticed? The enemy is trash-talking God. If you are a Christian, that should tick you off. As a believer, the Holy Spirit has anointed you with power to take on giants. Think about what God has done for you in the past. It will give you confidence that He will also act now and in the future.

COMPETITIVE GREATNESS
Be at your best when your best is needed.
Enjoyment of a difficult challenge.

Your Turn

■ Read 1 Samuel 16:1—17:58; 1 Corinthians 9:24-27; and Ephesians 6:10-17.

■ List a few times when you have boldly stood up for God. Were these events in the distant past or are they more current? Is your boldness increasing or decreasing? If you need more boldness, how are you going to go about obtaining it?

❑ I commit myself to giving my all for God.

Almighty Father in heaven, give me a competitive spirit so that I might successfully defend the faith and unite believers in the battle for souls. Whenever I falter, remind me of what You have done for me in the past so that my courage will be built up for the future. Thank You.

AMBITION

WOODEN

To hold a structure of bricks (or blocks) together, the mason applies mortar around each layer. In the Pyramid of Success, character qualities bond the 15 building blocks, thus symbolizing mortar. These character qualities actually run throughout the Pyramid and help us advance toward the apex.

Except for faith and patience (which I place at the top of the Pyramid), the other bonding agents can be moved and still support the Pyramid. Actually, I have shifted the order through the years, but I've come to prefer the arrangement I use in this book. Let's start with ambition.

Ambition is a feeling or a desire to achieve a goal. Usually that goal revolves around a person's definition of success or greatness. I believe we are most likely to succeed when ambition is focused on noble and worthy purposes and outcomes rather than on goals set out of selfishness. If our ambition is to be highly publicized, receive a lot of recognition, attain a position of power or prestige or make a lot of money, we do not have noble goals. If we are focused away from ourselves and on the team, God and others, we possess noble goals.

When we have noble goals, we prioritize the bigger picture. As a result, people with noble goals tend to bring the team and others along with them while they climb the Pyramid of Success.

> For wherever there is jealousy and selfish ambition, there you will find disorder and every kind of evil (Jas. 3:16).

CARTY

Once upon a time there was a guy who climbed to the top of the heap, but lost by a hair. It's a tragic story of selfish ambition run amuck.

Absalom had his half brother murdered (see 2 Sam. 13:1—18:18), then hid for three years. When he returned home, his father—King David gave him the cold shoulder. This did not set well with the ambitious Absalom, so he decided to get even by replacing his father as king.

To impress the crowds, Absalom rode a chariot with 50 outriders. His good looks and flowing long hair wowed the people. His clever, silver-tongued speech swayed them. Absalom's subversive plan was so effective that he pulled off a bloodless coup, overthrew his dad, and had himself crowned king.

David put off a confrontation as long as possible, but eventually he and his army had to battle his son. Twenty thousand people died in the skirmish, including Absalom. It seems that while retreating, Absalom's hair got wrapped in a tree, but his mount kept going. One of David's men found the would-be king dangling from the tree and shish-kebabed him three times. Thus, Absalom suffered the consequences of his selfish ambition.

AMBITION
(For noble goals)

Your Turn

- ■ Read 2 Samuel 13:1—18:18; Romans 12:1-2; and James 3:13—4:10.

- ■ List the current driving forces in your life. How much of your ambition in these areas is self-centered and how much is noble? Do you need to rethink and redirect any of your goals? What will be your first steps to change?

- ❑ I commit myself to putting aside selfish goals and to setting new, noble goals that will help other people and bring glory to God.

Almighty God and heavenly Father, show me if selfish ambition is getting in the way of our relationship and help me to set noble goals that will be pleasing in Your sight and bring glory to You. Thank You.

SINCERITY

WOODEN

Friendship, loyalty, cooperation and team spirit each occupy building blocks in the Pyramid of Success. These blocks underscore the fact that we cannot become successful unless we interact with others. Sincerity is the mortar that binds together the blocks of friendship, loyalty, cooperation and team spirit, and is therefore necessary to reach the apex.

Sincerity may not help us make friends, but it will help us keep them. It often takes time to be validated by others, but once a person knows that our word, character and steadfastness will withstand the tests of life, a firm friendship can be established and maintained.

Like anyone else, I have people in my life who don't like me or who disagree with certain things I do. When I have become aware of a problem or disagreement, I have attempted reconciliation. I have reached out in all sincerity; yet, in some cases, it has been to no avail.

Having people in our lives who are alienated from us doesn't mean that we can't be successful. However, there is a caution: if we find that it is the norm for us to leave people floating, drifting and drowning like debris in our wake, we aren't a success, regardless of the recognition the world gives us. Without sincerity, we will alienate people needlessly. With sincerity, we will have an abundance of friends and be one step closer to success.

The purpose of my instruction is that all the Christians there would be filled with love that comes from a pure heart, a clear conscience, and sincere faith (1 Tim. 1:5).

CARTY

The word "sincerely" means "without wax." It comes from the Latin words *sine cera*. Roman potters would take vessels that had hairline cracks and fill the gaps with wax. In time, the wax would melt and the vessel would leak. Potential buyers would hold pottery to the light to look for cracks filled with wax.

Commercially, the practice of filling in mistakes with wax became so commonplace that a tested vessel (a container held up to the light) was called "sincere," or without wax. Biblically, the concept translates as without blemish, pure, wholesome, genuine, true or sincere. Yet we are sinners. When exposed to the light of Jesus, we all have cracks! Jesus is the only one who can fill the cracks, but He does not do it with wax. He does it with something more permanent—His blood.

Increasing control over temptation and rushing back to God when we do sin are two good measurements of a sincere faith. After we confess our sin and ask for forgiveness, Jesus applies the power of His blood to our cracks, making us as without wax. Only in this way can we become more sincere as believers.

SINCERITY
(Keeps friends)

YOUR TURN

■ Read Matthew 11:7-11; 14:1-12; Mark 6:14-29; John 3:22-30; and Hebrews 10:22.

■ When you sin, how fast do you go to God and ask for forgiveness? What can you do to reduce the number of cracks in your life and become more waxless?

❑ I commit myself to becoming a sincere person in every area of my life, even when there is a cost.

Dear Father of faith, I want my faith to be sincere. Forgive me of my sins and help me gain a greater measure of control over my fallen nature through the power of Your Holy Spirit. And Lord, give me a passion to stay in Your will for increasing periods of time. Thank You.

ADAPTABILITY

WOODEN

Adaptability is being able to adjust to any situation at any given time. In life, we can only be sure of a few things, such as death and taxes. We can also count on change. We need to recognize change, grow with it and learn from it.

Since change is inevitable, inflexible people will never reach the apex of the Pyramid. If we want to succeed, we must adapt to circumstances as they unfold, including both conditions that we cannot change and those that will take time to change.

Life itself underscores this dynamic. When our parents take us out of our crib and stand us upright, we must adapt by trying to take our first steps or we will fall down. As teens, we must adjust to one bodily change after another. As adults, we adapt to changes such as going to college, getting a job, getting married, having children, sending our children off to college, having grandchildren, retiring and so forth. Each season brings about change, much of which we cannot control. If we fail to adapt, we fail to move forward.

To take advantage of changing circumstances, we must survey our situation and then adjust. We can plan a road trip or a workday down to the last detail, but the unexpected will always arise. If we are not malleable, we will get left behind.

To the weak I became weak, that I
might win the weak; I have become all
things to all men, that I may by all
means save some (1 Cor. 9:22, *NASB*).

CARTY

In biblical days, most outsiders hated the Jewish
people, whom God had chosen as His prize. The
Jewish people were equally bigoted. As they saw
it, there were two groups: the Jews and every-
body else.

Jesus broke this barrier many times, such as
when he had dinner with sinners. His social no
no caused a stir, especially among legalistic Jews
known as the Pharisees. Among Jesus' followers,
however, only Peter and Paul figured out that
Jesus wanted them to adapt and change their
attitude toward Gentiles. The apostle Paul took
the adjusting one step further when he declared,
"There is no longer Jew or Gentile, slave or free,
male or female. For you are all Christians—you
are one in Christ Jesus" (Gal. 3:28).

Adapting may mean adjusting to an opponent's full-court press in a basketball game, or it
may mean changing an ingrained belief because
God wants us to move forward. Whether the
issue is small or large, humdrum or close to our
hearts, the ability to adapt is a vital cohesion in
holding together the blocks of the Pyramid.

ADAPTABILITY

(to any situation)

Your Turn

■ Read Acts 10:1-48; 15:6-11; 1 Corinthians 9:20-22; and Galatians 2:1-10; 3:23—4:7.

■ What criteria do you use to determine when you need to adapt? List a few significant times in which you adapted, even if you did so reluctantly. How do you respond when God asks you to adjust a habit, attitude or behavioral pattern in your life?

❏ I commit myself to being an instrument of change for truth and righteousness even in circumstances requiring me to change my thinking.

*Dear Creator of all people, open my eyes
to the changes I need to make in my life. I want
to adapt to be all things to all people so that I might
be able to effectively share Your truth with those
You place in my path. Thank You.*

HONESTY

WOODEN

Honesty is doing what we know is right and not giving into the temptation to do what we know is wrong. Honesty must occur at all times, in both our thoughts and actions. Honest people stay on the narrow way, regardless of the consequences. If we are honest, our integrity will not allow us to compromise—ever. Honest people simply don't lie to others, themselves or God.

A dishonest act is an attempt to deceive someone. It is possible to be so deceptive that we even fool ourselves. We do this when we attempt to justify a lie because of circumstances or as payback. Dishonesty—no matter the reason—destroys our credibility, reputation and self-respect.

I have been tempted to be dishonest many times. I have mostly resisted these temptations, but one particular time I failed. An opposing coach repeatedly sent the wrong shooter to the free-throw line. He would slip in a player with a better shooting percentage than the one who was fouled. Since he got away with this illegal maneuver, I tried it, too. But I was not so good at being stealthy—and I got caught. I regret giving in to temptation not only because I got caught, but because I did not stay true to my standards.

Telling the truth not only enhances our relations with others and with God, it makes us feel good about ourselves.

Remember, it is sin to know what you ought to do and then not do it (Jas. 4:17).

CARTY

At one time or another each of us is tempted to mislead, lie or cheat. We usually don't have a lot to say about when the temptation will come—thoughts just pop into our mind and situations just appear. We can even hoodwink ourselves with sneaky justifications, such as *No one will notice* or *A little white lie will not hurt anyone* or *Everyone does it!*

Simply having a thought is not a problem, but giving it room to grow is. We can control whether we dwell upon a particular temptation or vanquish it. The longer we hold on to a thought, the more likely we are to act upon it. Staying honest is as simple as discerning between good thoughts and bad thoughts and not allowing the bad ones to linger.

Much of being honest has to do with self-respect. Deep down, we know when we have lied. Basic truth telling is vital to success. Without it, the Pyramid cannot stand upright. However, when we look deeper into this quality, we find the need to be honest with God and ourselves in all circumstances, no matter the cost.

HONESTY
(in thought and action)

YOUR TURN

- Read Acts 2:1-41; 4:1-22; Matthew 28:19-20; and John 20:21.

- Think about the last time you were tempted to cheat. What were the circumstances? Did you try to justify it? Did you dwell on the temptation or chase it away? Why did you react the way you reacted? Do you need to change the way you deal with the temptation to cheat?

- ☐ I commit myself to being honest with others, myself and God.

Almighty God, give me the courage to stand up for You even when it is difficult. I want to be honest with You and true to myself. Through the power of Your Holy Spirit, help me to stay faithful, even in the face of persecution. Thank You.

RESOURCEFULNESS

WOODEN

Resourcefulness is using our wits, proper judgment and common sense to solve problems and meet challenges. It is using initiative in difficult situations, and it involves inventing, creating, imagining, synthesizing, evaluating, classifying, observing and analyzing solutions to overcome the trials that life throws at us. Resourcefulness is dreaming up ways to meet our goals.

Some of my greatest pleasures have come from finding ways to overcome obstacles. One of the most resourceful times of my life came while I was at Indiana State, where I wore too many hats. I was the athletic director, the head basketball coach, the head baseball coach, a teacher and a graduate student, all at the same time. There were times when I felt like a plate spinner on the old *Ed Sullivan Show*, working hard to keep all those plates spinning on those sticks. If I wanted to get anything done, I had to be resourceful.

I look back on it now and wonder how I did it. I guess I know. Some of the things I didn't get done very well. But that doesn't mean I wasn't resourceful or successful. Actually, it was one of the most successful times of my life. I was making the effort to do my best. Remember, results aren't the criteria for success—it's the effort made for achievement that is most important. Being resourceful takes effort.

So I tell you, keep on asking, and you will be given what you ask for. Keep on looking, and you will find. Keep on knocking, and the door will be opened (Luke 11:9).

CARTY

I have a favorite saying: *We get what we need when we need it—when we ask for it.* When our will matches God's will and we ask for help, we get what we need. The secret is to match our will with God's will. That occurs when we move closer to God. The Lord says, "I will guide you along the best pathway for your life. I will advise you and watch over you" (Ps. 32:8). God guides us through His Holy Spirit, which is the best resource of all.

When I get stuck on a problem, I first make sure that my sin is confessed. That aligns me with God. Next I review the situation, pray and go to bed. When I wake up the next morning, an insight is often there. Given a little more time—after my wits are tempered with sound judgment, common sense, the guidance of the Holy Spirit and prayer—a solution usually comes.

God will never let us be challenged without giving us the tools we need to do the job or solve the problem. We may have to scramble to put those tools to work, but that's where resourcefulness comes in.

RESOURCEFULNESS
(proper judgment)

YOUR TURN

- Read 1 Samuel 21:10—22:2; Psalm 32:8; Proverbs 31:10-31; Luke 11:5-13; and John 14:12-18.

- Can you remember an incident when you used creative or unconventional thinking to solve a problem? What was the key to finding the solution? Can you remember a time when prayer and the leading of the Holy Spirit clearly provided an answer to a problem?

❑ I commit myself to using all of the resources God has given me so that creative solutions can be found for the problems I face.

Dear Creator of all resources, I desire to put all that You have given me to work for Your honor and glory. Help me to rely on You for solutions to all the problems and challenges of life. Teach me to pray and follow the leading of Your Spirit. Thank You for Your guidance. Amen.

JOURNAL ENTRY
MORTAR QUALITY 5:
RESOURCEFULNESS

RELIABILITY

WOODEN

When we are reliable, others know that they can depend on us. They know that we will make the effort to do our best, whatever the situation might be. They know we won't run, cower or become paralyzed by fear. They have learned to count on our consistency and trustworthiness. We'll still be there making the effort to do our best long after weaker people have faded. Reliability earns the respect of those around us.

Curtis Rowe was one of my most reliable players. Although he usually wasn't spectacular, he consistently played at a very high level. I could have almost penciled in his stat line before the game began. It was a rarity for him not to perform well, and I came to count on him.

Capability has nothing to do with reliability. Some people don't have as much capability as others have, but they make up for it by being reliable. Mark Madsen comes to mind. He isn't as capable as many NBA players, but he gets closer to giving you all he has to give more consistently than most of his contemporaries. The coach and his teammates both know what to expect from him every night. Though he isn't as capable as some he is always reliable, which makes him valuable to his team.

If we are going to be successful, we must first be reliable.

So Achish called David and said to him, "As surely as the LORD lives, you have been reliable, and I would be pleased to have you serve with me in the army" (1 Sam. 29:6).

CARTY

Barnabas wasn't flashy, but he was reliable (see Acts 13:1; 14:14). He proved himself when Saul, the persecutor of Christians, converted and became the apostle Paul. Many believers were skeptical regarding his conversion (see Acts 9:26). Not Barnabas. Mr. Reliable went to see Paul, hung out at Starbucks with him, got a sense of his potential and brought him back to the church at Antioch. Barnabas discipled Paul for a year and then set him loose to become arguably the most famous apostle. That was fine with Barnabas. By the time the two men were charged to take money to the famine-stricken poor in Jerusalem, it was Paul who directed the trip.

Barnabas was strong and dependable. He became a nobody in order to make other nobodies somebodies. Whether God calls us to discipleship (like Barnabas) or missions (like Paul), He should be able to pencil in our stats ahead of time. He must be able to rely upon us to fulfill our calling. If we are not reliable, we will never be all that God wants us to be.

RELIABILITY
(creates respect)

YOUR TURN

- Read Acts 9:19-31; 13:1-13; 15:36-40; and 2 Timothy 4:9.

- Among the people you know, who are the most dependable? Why do you consider them to be so reliable? List some of the ways people depend on you. Are you more (or less) dependable now than in the past? How can you become a more reliable person?

- ☐ I commit myself to keeping my word and to being there for others when they most need help.

Almighty Father, thank You that You are in the business of rescuing the wounded. Bind my hurts, heal me and direct me to the ministry You have planned for me. I want to be Your reliable servant, for Jesus' sake. I want You to be able to pencil in my stats ahead of time. Amen.

FIGHT

WOODEN

Fight is a determined effort to do the very best we can do. On the basketball court, fight is measured by hustle: diving to the floor for loose balls, sprinting to fill a lane on a fast break, taking a charge, picking up a missed defensive assignment or stealing the ball from an opposing player. It's digging in, gritting our teeth and standing our ground.

When we have fight, we are always ready to respond. We are quick, but we don't hurry. We make fewer mistakes because we have the level of our intensity under control. Players with fight have a contained fire burning in their bellies, which emerges as focused passion. Players with fight never lose a game; they just run out of time.

Fight has some negative connotations that I don't want to communicate. In no way is this mortar quality about an opponent. There was a time when I would talk about "being better than the opponent." I don't anymore. Make no mistake, I always want to win, but I never fight with an opponent. My fight is within me—it is the struggle to be the best I can be at whatever I do. In basketball, if both teams play up to their potential, only one will win—but both will be winners. If we use our fight to do our best, success will take care of itself.

I have fought the good fight, I have finished the race, I have kept the faith
(2 Tim. 4:7).

CARTY

Paul knew how to fight right. The apostle was
preaching in Iconium when some naysayers
took offense to the message about the Messiah.
Paul and his cohort Barnabas fled to Lystra,
where they were mistaken for Greek gods. They
tried to straighten the record and preached
about Jesus—*then troublemakers from Iconium
arrived in Lystra*. The Iconiumers wanted to fight
the wrong way, and they stoned Paul.

After being stoned, the apostle was dragged
out of town, where wild dogs were expected to
finish the job. However, before the dogs were
able to find him, Paul dug deep inside himself
and found the energy to walk back to Lystra,
where he spent the night. The next day he started the next leg of his missionary journey—a 60-
mile trek to the city of Derbe.

Fourteen years later, Paul wrote about the
experience (see 1 Cor. 12:2). He thought that
he had died, seen heaven and been healed.
Whatever happened, it certainly took everything
he had to take that first step toward Derbe. But
nothing could keep Paul from giving his best
effort for the cause of Christ—not even being the
object of the wrong kind of fight. He was determined and knew how to fight the good fight.

FIGHT
(determined effort)

YOUR TURN

■ Read Acts 14:8-20 and 1 Corinthians 12:2-10.

■ Describe a time in your life when you fought a good fight but came in second. How were you a winner in that situation? Describe a time in your life when a situation forced you to dig deeper within yourself than you knew you could dig. What did you discover about determination? What does this have to do with knowing how to fight what 2 Timothy 4:7 calls "the good fight"?

❑ I commit myself to fighting the good fight, finishing the race and keeping the faith.

Heavenly Father, I want to give You the best effort of which I am capable of giving. I want to worship You with all of my heart. I want to represent You with all of the zeal of which I am capable. Help me to fight the good fight. Thank You.

INTEGRITY

WOODEN

To some extent, integrity contains reliability, honesty and sincerity. However, in its simplest form, integrity is purity of intention. It's keeping a clean conscience. Purity of intention is really a reflection of the heart. People with integrity always want to do what's right—once they are sure what "right" is.

The Lord created each of us to be unique, but I believe that He put some absolutes in place. The Ten Commandments reflect some of these absolutes. When we violate them, we fail as people of integrity. Being true to ourselves doesn't make us people of integrity. Charles Manson was true to himself, and as a result, he rightly is spending the rest of his life in prison. Ultimately, being true to our Creator is what produces the purest form of integrity.

People with integrity do what is right both on and off the court. I had great basketball players who fell short. They had what I call "selective integrity." In basketball situations, I could count on them. They were reliable and they were sincerely committed to the team. Some were even on my NCAA championship teams, but they were not successful in my way of thinking. They did not carry over their integrity into every other area of their lives. As a result, their selective integrity kept them from becoming all they were capable of becoming.

There was a man named Job who lived
in the land of Uz. He was blameless, a
man of complete integrity. He feared
God and stayed away from evil (Job 1:1).

CARTY

The top five on God's integrity list are Jesus,
John the Baptist, Noah, Daniel and Job. How do
I know? The Bible tells us so.

Jesus is the obvious choice for number one.
He's perfect and never sinned. John the Baptist
is second because Jesus called him the greatest
person ever born (see Matt. 11:11). God Himself
named the next three: Noah, Daniel and Job
(see Ezek. 14:14).

Where does Mary, the mother of Jesus, fit?
We know that she was blessed above all women
(see Luke 1:42), but even Jesus didn't rank her
above John the Baptist. Since the Bible is silent
on this matter, I will slide her in at number
three. I know—that puts six people on a list of
five. Whoever said basketball players could
count? Besides, the order of the final three (uh,
four) does not really matter.

Where you fit doesn't matter either. When
it comes to having integrity, God does not keep
a top-five list. What matters most are the core
commitments that define you as a person. Is
there consistency between your words and
actions, thoughts and choices, and values and
behaviors? Are you a person of integrity?

INTEGRITY
(purity of intention)

Your Turn

- Read Genesis 6:8-9; Ezekiel 14:14; Daniel 1:8-16; Matthew 11:11; 22:16; Luke 1:39-55; and Romans 3:21-26; 4:3.

- What is it about John the Baptist, Noah, Daniel, Job and Mary that make them people of integrity? Who are the top five people of integrity that you know? Why have you put each on the list? Would any of your friends put you on their top-five list? What do you need to do to increase the purity of intention in your life?

- ❏ I commit myself to becoming a better representative of Jesus Christ.

Gracious God of purity, I want my intentions to be pure and my actions to be consistent with my core value of bringing glory to Your holy name. I want to be a person of impeccable integrity. Guard me against compromise. May there be absolutely no disparity between what I say and what I do. Amen.

PATIENCE

WOODEN

Patience is the ability to wait and persevere. Think about the fun of Christmas. Why can't children get to sleep on Christmas Eve? Anticipation! The waiting heightens the joy everyone experiences the next morning.

Good things take time, as they should. We shouldn't expect good things to happen overnight. Actually, getting something too easily or too soon can cheapen the outcome. For example, people who inherit a lot of money frequently don't appreciate it and cannot handle its value. Many end up broke and disillusioned.

Young people can be impatient. They have a tendency to want to change more things more quickly. The mistake they make is that they see all change as progress and fail to see the benefit of waiting.

As we grow older, we tend to get more patient. Things don't seem to be as urgent. But older people tend to forget that there is no progress without change. It is impossible to maintain the status quo; therefore, change is inevitable. An organization that is not changing is not moving forward. The question is how fast should change come?

The maxim *easy come, easy go* carries more truth than most people realize. When we add to our accomplishments the element of hard work over a long period of time, we'll place a far greater value on the outcome. When we are patient, we'll have a greater appreciation of our success.

Don't you realize how kind, tolerant, and patient God is with you? Or don't you care? Can't you see how kind he has been in giving you time to turn from your sin? (Rom. 2:4).

Carty

In Luke, we find the story of a dude who had 100 sheep (see Luke 15:4-7). One day, one of the sheep in the flock wandered away and the shepherd had to go on a search-and-rescue mission.

I never have understood why a responsible shepherd would put an entire flock at risk for one not-so-bright animal. Rustlers, coyotes and wolves could have had a field day with the unattended flock. Maybe the stray would wander back on its own. Why gamble? The downside risk was too great for such a small upside potential. At least the shepherd still had 99 sheep—that's the way I saw the situation.

But that's not the way God saw it. The 99 sheep represented those who believe in the one true God. What's the worst thing that could have happened to them? They could have been killed. What would have happened to them when they were dead? They would have gone to heaven. This does not trivialize life or death; rather, it reveals God's patience. The greatest concern, therefore, was for the lost one. God specializes in lost sheep. He is patient in the task of finding them. That's good news for lost sheep.

PATIENCE
(good things take time)

YOUR TURN

■ Read Luke 15:4-32.

■ Are you patient or do you want things to change quickly? Has your patience increased as you have grown older? Give an example of something you now wait to see happen that you might have been impatient to see happen when you were younger. How has God shown His patience with you?

❑ I commit to learn how to wait without being anxious. I want to learn patience.

Patient Father, thank You for never giving up on me. I want to come home and feel Your welcoming embrace. Amen.

FAITH

WOODEN

I served as a basketball coach at a public institution, where faith in God was not part of my curriculum. But I always included faith at the top of the Pyramid. In its basic form, the faith I taught my players to have was a faith that things would turn out for the best. I also encouraged my players to have a faith and to be able to defend it.

Although I was not vocal about my beliefs, I always had a Bible on my desk and I intentionally led by example, based on Christ's teaching. Rather than speaking about Jesus' principles, I just attempted to demonstrate them by the way I lived my life.

Some evangelical Christians think of me as being too liberal and some liberals consider me to be too conservative. I know we can't please everyone, so I haven't tried. I have only wanted to please God.

It was important to me to never come across as being critical of someone else's faith. As a result, I never tried to change a person's faith. I saw that as God's job, not mine. I did encourage my players to stay open-minded, however, because I felt that those who were open-minded would give way to truth and those who weren't wouldn't. I have always believed that what Christ said is truth, and that He is Truth.

Therefore, since we have been made right in God's sight by faith, we have peace with God because of what Jesus Christ our Lord has done for us (Rom. 5:1).

CARITY

Players who have faith are generally the most consistent in making the effort to become the best they can be. That works well on the basketball floor, but there is a bigger question about faith.

The Pyramid helps us become successful in life, no matter our faith. But the fruit of our lives won't solve the problem at our lives' end. I believe there will be good people who will not go to heaven because they didn't get the faith part right.

There are Hindus, Muslims, Scientologists, and so many more. The world is full of religions that claim to be the way; however, they can't all be right. Jesus said, "I am the way, the truth, and the life. No one can come to the Father except through me" (John 14:6).

If Jesus is wrong, then all the good people, no matter their faith, are on the right path. On the other hand, if He is right, everyone who doesn't know Him will end up separated from God, no matter how successful they are in life. Those who miss heaven can hardly be considered a success. The issue of eternity makes faith the most important principle in the Pyramid.

FAITH
(through prayer)

YOUR TURN

- Read John 14:1-12; Romans 3:21-28; 5:1-11; 2 Thessalonians 1:3-12; and James 2:14-26.

- Coach encouraged his players to have a faith and to be able to defend it. In what do you have faith and how do you defend it? If Jesus truly is the only way, how does this effect your perception of faith and its place in the Pyramid? How can you better work out this faith in your life?

- ☐ I commit to study the claims of Jesus Christ. I want to know if He really is the only way to God.

Dear God and Father of faith, I want to get this right. I want Jesus Christ to be my Lord and Savior. Amen.

SUCCESS

WOODEN

When do we know that we have succeeded? Is it when we have a mantel full of trophies? Is it when we have met our goals? Is it when we have a good reputation? When it comes to reaching the apex of the Pyramid, none of these factors matter. What we should be concerned about is our character. Our character represents what we truly are, while accolades and achievements are merely byproducts of what others perceive us to be.

Having attempted to give our all is what matters—and we are the only ones who really know the truth about our own capabilities and corresponding performance.

People still want to hear me speak and to meet with me, and I am honored by their requests. It is a privilege to be able to continue to encourage others. My family has been around me, too. I am blessed beyond belief—but am I a success?

I can recount so many blessings in my life and I am thankful for them, but blessings don't constitute success. If none of the good things had ever occurred, I would not be any less successful. The real determining factor is this: Did I make the effort to do my best? That is the only criteria, and I am the only one who knows (well, me and God).

Am I a success?

I have peace of mind.

Well done, my good and faithful servant (Matt. 25:21).

CARTY

Paul had peace of mind even though Nero would soon have his head. The apostle was in his early 60s when he wrote from the Mamertine prison in Rome to his friend and disciple, Timothy. Since Paul wasn't sure when he was going to die, he wanted Timothy to bring him a cloak before winter (see 2 Tim. 4:22).

Paul gave his all for God. He gave everything he had to every task. Although he occasionally stumbled, he didn't quit, drop out or give up. His faith never wavered. In every situation, he trusted God, served Christ and finished well. He knew that he would hear God say, "Well done, good and faithful servant." He had peace of mind.

On Earth, success is having peace of mind in knowing that we have done our best to become the best that we are capable of becoming. When we have this peace, we have reached the apex of the Pyramid of Success.

In eternity, success is having done our best to allow God to do His best in us and through us. When we live like this, we too will hear the words "Well done," and we too will have a peace that passes all understanding.

SUCCESS

Success is peace of mind that is a direct result of self-satisfaction in knowing you did your best to become the best you are capable of becoming.

YOUR TURN

■ Read Jeremiah 29:11-13; Matthew 25:14-30; and 2 Timothy 4:1-22.

■ Where are you on Coach Wooden's Pyramid of Success? List the Building Blocks and Mortar Qualities. Write a sentence about each one explaining how it is manifest (or not manifest) in your life. Which ones do you need to work on the most? Do you have the peace that passes all understanding? Will you hear the words "Well done"? What changes can you make in your life so that you can be all that God created you to be?

❑ I commit myself to putting aside selfish goals and to setting new noble goals that will help other people and bring glory to God.

*Great God and Author of plans, thank You
for Your plans for me. I want to live up to my
responsibilities in being all that You created me to be.
Grant to me the courage to make the effort to do
my best to become all that I can become to bring
glory to You and advance Your Kingdom. Father,
I long to hear You say, "Well done, my good and
faithful servant." May it be so.*

The Coach of the Century Reveals His Secret to Success

Coach Wooden's Pyramid of Success
Building Blocks for a Better Life
John Wooden and *Jay Carty*
ISBN 0830936794 • Hardcover

In *Coach Wooden's Pyramid of Success*, legendary college basketball coach John Wooden and Jay Carty reveal the building blocks and key values that have brought Coach Wooden to the pinnacle of success as a leader, a teacher and a follower of God. Each of the 27 daily readings takes an in-depth look at a single principle, which together with the other principles contribute to lifelong success in *every* area of life.

Pick Up a Copy at Your Favorite Bookstore!

God's Word for Your World

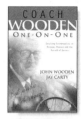

**Coach Wooden
One-on-One**
Inspiring Conversations on
Purpose, Passion and
the Pursuit of Success
*John Wooden
and Jay Carty*
ISBN 08307.32918

**The 5 Secrets to
Becoming a Leader**
Words of Wisdom for
the Untrained Leader
*Alan Nelson
and Stan Toler*
ISBN 08307.29151

**The Unquenchable
Worshipper**
Coming Back to the Heart
of Worship
Matt Redman
ISBN 08307.29135

**The Measure
of a Man**
Twenty Attributes
of a Godly Man
Gene A. Getz
ISBN 08307.34953

Pick Up a Copy at Your Favorite Bookstore!

Regal
God's Word for Your World™
www.regalbooks.com

FOR MORE INFORMATION
JAY CARTY
1033 NEWTON ROAD
SANTA BARBARA, CA 93103

WWW.JAYCARTY.COM
JAY@JAYCARTY.COM